BY KATHY AND AMY ELDON

D1487482

Love Catcher

Inviting
love into
your life

A journal

CHRONICLE BOOKS
SAN FRANCISCO

DEDICATION

To the frogs and princes who teach us how to love

ISBN: 0-8118-4915-5

Manufactured in China

Visit www.creativevisions.org to find out more about
the work of Kathy and Amy Eldon.

Design: Eliza F. Mayo

Typeset in Koch Antiqua and Goudy Sans

Distributed in Canada by

Raincoast Books

9050 Shaughnessy Street

Vancouver, B.C. V6P 6E5

10 9 8 7 6 5 4 3 2 1

Chronicle Books LLC

85 Second Street

San Francisco, CA 94105

www.chroniclebooks.com

CONTENTS

We all need to be loved. Everyone wants to be listened to, nurtured, cherished, and adored. Some of us long for romance, while others want a companion or someone special to give us backrubs and hugs. Many are anxious for a rebirth in an old relationship or guidance to help separate from a partner in the most loving way possible. We want to love our children and our parents, to be good friends and family members. In an increasingly complex and fast-moving world, we long to be part of an interconnected, caring community.

We all want more love in our lives, but most of us don't know where to find it and usually look in all the wrong places! We don't realize that to be loved, we must learn to love. To receive love, we must give it—not only to others, but also to ourselves. We don't have to rely on anyone else, for inside each one of us is an infinite source of loving energy. We just have to open the tap and allow it to flow through us.

It is then that we discover that love is everywhere. Love is in the infinite mysteries of nature and the miracle of simply being alive. Love is in old friends and new, in momentary encounters with strangers, in the magic of rediscovering our creativity, exercising our bodies, or stretching our minds. Love is in a gesture, a silent prayer, a gift of appreciation, or a phone call. Give love away, and you will find it pouring back.

Love Catcher has been created to help you learn how to attract vibrant, new love into every aspect of your life. Most importantly, our book will enable you to truly love yourself. The journal provides a framework for you to examine your own life and relationship to love. It will help you discover what has shaped you in the past and will help you to listen to the wisdom of your own inner voice to create a glorious new future which will embrace love in every possible way. Invite love into your life. Begin it now!

HOW TO USE LOVE CATCHER

There are no rules for using *Love Catcher*! It's for your eyes only, unless you want to share your thoughts with someone special. Answer the questions on paper or in your head, draw or doodle in the journal, and glue in clippings or photographs. Do whatever it takes to help you to uncover your true thoughts and feelings on all aspects of love. Whatever you do, keep the book in a safe place or tear out the pages you don't want others to see.

If you wish, begin with "**History of My Heart**," which explores how you became who you are today. Who or what shaped your views and attitudes on love? What was the nature of your parents' relationship? Are there romantic patterns from the past you wish to change? Old scripts you should leave behind? Do you feel worthy of receiving more love in your life? If not, why not? And most importantly, what is blocking you from attracting the love you want into your life?

Turn to chapter two, "**Ready to Love**," to help you prepare your body, mind, and spirit to receive the right love into your life. Use this section to focus on YOU, as you ready yourself for the exciting prospect of meeting a person who will love you for who you really are, not the person you would like to be (or pretend you are). The exercises in this section will provide the tools and inspiration for you to become totally alive to life and love, with all its possibilities.

Chapter three, "**Fire and Desire**," will guide you through the magical, crazy days of a new love, when we daydream, bump into walls, stop eating, and yearn for the next encounter. This chapter will help you keep your feet on the ground as you explore the nature of your relationship, while compiling a delicious record of this exciting time.

Chapter four, "**Conscious Loving**," will help you get the most out of the early stages of loving by offering tips on how to clearly communicate your needs and feelings, while listening to and supporting your partner. This section will help you lay a strong foundation of wisdom and understanding as you work through issues in a loving way, instead of getting stuck in old scripts and useless battles.

"**Beyond the Butterflies**" offers new insight into a relationship that has moved beyond the fairy-tale aspects of new love into the more challenging time that inevitably sets in after the honeymoon period is over. The questions in this section will help you deal with the disillusionment and disappointment we feel as we discover aspects of the other person that fall short of our expectations. The questions in this section will allow for the release of feelings of anger, frustration, heartache, and doubt, which are also part of the journey to real loving.

"**Dark Nights**" provides insight into the really difficult periods we encounter in relationships, times when we wonder if we can ever rekindle the love we once shared with our partners. This section will help you mend a broken relationship or, if necessary, separate from your partner in the most loving way possible.

"**Rebirth of Love**" is designed to transform a tired relationship into a vital new experience of loving, as you revive the body, mind, and soul connection between you and your partner. It's a time of taking stock, forgiving, dreaming new dreams, and just plain having fun, while you rediscover why you fell in love in the first place.

As you work through *Love Catcher*, know, above all, that love is everywhere around you. Most of all, love is within you, aching to be expressed. Open yourself to love! Allow yourself to be free to experience abundance in every aspect of your life. Connect yourself to the powerful energy that surrounds and flows through us all, and celebrate the joy and peace you will feel as you infuse your life with love.

Love is, above all, a gift of oneself.
— Jean Anouilh, *Ardèle*

We are all products of our upbringing. We are the sum total of every relationship we have ever experienced, from our parents and siblings, friends and colleagues, to old lovers, our spouses, children—even strangers or casual acquaintances, whose words can make us glow, or leave hurt in our hearts long after we have forgotten their names or faces. We are the outcome of myths and misconceptions, the consequence of culturally imposed limitations and restrictions. We are often confused and usually confined by the expectation that we must lead the lives of someone else's choice.

The exciting news is that we can change! We can evolve, grow, burst out of old patterns and boundaries to embrace a brand-new way of being that allows for a glorious flow of love in and through our lives.

It's just a question of deciding that you want to grow out of the old and welcome the new you.

In this section, we ask you to examine the old patterns of behavior, which have created your expectations of who and how you should love. Don't be afraid to be totally honest. This is your book. Put it under lock and key if necessary. Dig deeply into your thoughts and feelings as you fill in these pages. Examine the past to reveal old patterns that you want to leave behind. Visualize new ways of behaving which will more appropriately reflect the person you are today. Resolve to leave behind fear, as you begin to live your life from a place of love.

Know that as you express the truth of who you are and what you wish for in your life, your heart will open, and love will start to flow through you. You will begin to forgive, knowing that everything that has happened in your life so far has provided opportunities for your growth. Few of us welcome the hard times, but they are behind you. This is NOW—a time of new beginnings.

Above all, remember that you are connected to divine energy—the only source of love. You are love. You are the infinite flow of love in your life—and need only to open the floodgates of your heart and say yes.

HISTORY OF MY HEART

My first love

My greatest love

My heartbreak

My greatest lesson

My last love

My future love

It is said you are often attracted to partners who share characteristics, both positive and negative, of your mother or father.

My mother's good traits

My mother's not-so-good traits

My father's good traits

My father's not-so-good traits

How does my partner compare?

My partner's good traits

My partner's not-so-good traits

PAST PARTNERS

What characteristics have my past partners shared?

Is there a pattern here?

Is it healthy?

If it isn't, what can I do to change it?

These are my role models when it comes to relationships

Here is why

How can I be more like those I respect?

AIM HIGH

My ideal partner will have these qualities

My ideal me would have these qualities

Here's what I need to work on

Sometimes I act differently depending on whom I'm with.

Sometimes I lose myself and forget who I really am.

When I was with _____ , I was

When I was with _____ , I was

When I was with _____ , I was

Now I am with my partner, I want to stay true to myself.

I need to

REVIEWS

In past relationships my partners have said mean things that I can't get out of my head.

Why is it so much easier to believe the bad things people say?

I want to remember my good qualities.

I am

I can't stop thinking about

It's driving me crazy, and it's holding me back from a healthy relationship with someone new.

I need to move on.

As hard as it is, I will try to forgive and to let go of the past.

I will begin by

FROGS

I keep falling for the wrong person.

Sometimes it feels like I am meeting the same person over and over again.

They have these characteristics in common

Next time I will be more aware of

I hate feeling rejected.

Here's what happened

It made me feel

What can I do to feel better?

GREENER GRASS

Why do I always want what I can't have?

What would happen if I could really have what I think I want?

Would I still want it?

I ache inside.

I want someone who doesn't want me.

I can make a choice.

I can keep yearning.

I can let go and open up to the possibility of another love.

I choose to

I will begin by

PATTERNS

Sometimes I feel like I keep making the same wrong choices over and over in my life.

I am repeating a pattern that isn't good for me.

I must try to be aware of what I am doing and break this cycle.

I will begin by

I am going to write a letter to my previous love. I have unresolved issues that could stand in the way of a future relationship.

When I am done, I will burn the letter and start all over again!

Dear _____ ,

FEEL THE FEAR (AND DO IT ANYWAY)

Why am I so scared about being vulnerable?

Here's who hurt me in the past

Here's how I dealt with it

Here's how I would handle it now

It is said, "You can't look; you can only find."

Am I looking too hard?

Will I terrify people with my desperate need to be with someone?

How can I trust that I will find the right person for me?

I will release and let go.

DESIRE

I want

I yearn for

I ache

I adore

I need

I crave

I have spent so much of my life looking outside myself for love.

I realize now I have been looking in all the wrong places.

I must trust that I am a source of love.

I will open myself to the flow of love in my life.

I will begin by

You say you are ready to love, but are you really? Are you ready to give love as well as receive it? Ready to open your heart, your mind, and your spirit to someone who loves you simply because you are who you are? Do you believe you are loveable? Able to be loved? A person worthy of the finest, kindest, most nourishing love imaginable?

After a lifetime of thinking of others first, it can be very difficult to turn the tables and love your own body, mind, and spirit. With practice though, you will see that once you glow with love from inside, you will find love flowing back. There is nothing more appealing than a person radiating love. Mahatma Gandhi once said, "Be the change you wish to see." You must give love—to yourself as well as others—in order to receive love.

It's hard to attract someone to love you if you feel like a shriveled-up flower inside. Flowers need nourishment to bloom. Our bodies, minds, and spirits do, too. If you have been neglecting your body, try to eat properly, take vitamins, and treat yourself to a facial or massage. Exercise, go for walks, drink lots of water, and rest.

Use this time to stretch your mind. Take classes, work on your memory, join the public library. Be brave! Hijack yourself and go on an adventure. Live the life you always wanted to live and see who you will meet along the way!

Just like your body and your mind, your soul needs nourishment, too. Feed it every day. Meditate, pray, take long walks, garden, or just take time out to listen to music; for it is when you are still and receptive that you can hear the wisdom of your inner voice.

It is said we attract at our own level, so be sure you are reflecting the very best of who you are, so you can bring the best possible person to you. Be alive to life! As you become clearer as to who you really are and express yourself with clarity and truth, you will find new energy beginning to flow through you. You will begin to glow with a radiant light from within. As your light shines more brightly, your presence will magnetize others. Starting now, connect to the source of love; express love, be love, and watch miracles begin to blossom in your life.

SOUL MATE

I want to attract someone with similar values in life.

What matters to me?

I want a partner who cares about

I want a partner who shares my beliefs in

I want a partner who is

○ compassionate

○ kind

○ loving

○ aware

○ forgiving

○ caring

○ positive

If I expect all these qualities, then I must develop them in myself.

I will begin by

Do I feel worthy of love?

If not, why not?

What can I do to feel okay about myself?

I will begin by

To love oneself is the beginning of
a lifelong romance.
— Oscar Wilde, *An Ideal Husband*

MIRRORS

It is said that what you give out is what you will receive.

What am I giving?

What am I receiving?

What do I need to change?

I will begin by

If you be loved, be worthy of love.
— Ovid

Who am I really?

What do I want to do in life?

Can I be who I really am?

Can I do what I wish to do?

Can I commit to be with someone who loves me for who I am?

To be true to myself I need to

I will begin by

PIE CHART

If I look at my life as a pie chart, here's how much time I spend on

– work

– hobbies

– relationship

– spiritual/religious

– volunteering

– family

– physical

– self-improvement

– learning

– friends

– other

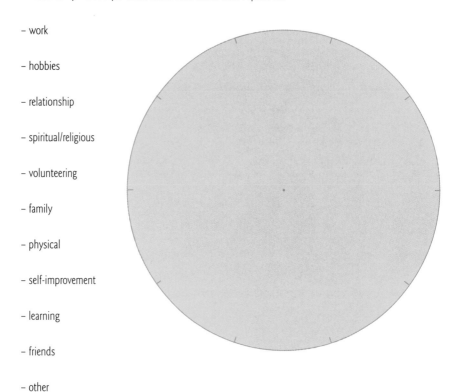

Am I in balance? Where do I need to spend more time?

Less time?

I will begin by

When I prepare for a job interview, I read, research, and try to look my best.

Now I must do the same to prepare myself for a partner.

Here are my strengths

Here are my weaknesses

Here is what I can reasonably expect to improve

I will begin by

GIVING

Sometimes I become completely self-absorbed and forget to look around me.

I will feel better if I can give something back instead of taking all the time.

I want to give

I will begin by

It is said that you should live as though every day were your last and learn like you'll live forever. There's so much in the world I want to know. It seems like there's never enough time to read, study, or expand my mind.

I'm going to make time to

Here's what I will focus on

I will start by

BEGIN IT NOW!

I am committed to

The worst thing that can happen is

I will begin by

They can
Because they think
They can.
— Virgil

I know I have an inner voice.

I just don't listen to it very often, and I am not always good at trusting my intuition.

Here is what it is saying right now

From this moment on, I promise I will listen carefully to my inner voice and try to act on what I hear.

CHERISHING

I want to be loved.

I want to be cherished.

I want to be adored.

I want

The question is, Why should I wait for someone else to love, cherish, and adore me?

I will celebrate myself by finding special ways to give myself the feelings I want from someone else.
As I begin to feel loved, cherished, and adored—by myself—I will not feel so "needy" about getting what
I need from someone else.

I know I am here for a reason.

So far I have done

Now it's time to

I will begin by

ATTRACTIONS

In the past I have been attracted to

I have attracted

What sort of person do I really want to attract?

I wish I were

In the past, maybe instead of trying to cultivate those characteristics in myself, I have looked for a partner to fill in the gaps. It's not fair to expect someone else to complete me.

I need to focus on developing qualities I ask for in someone else.

I will begin by

AFFIRMATIONS

I am beautiful.

I am kind.

I am strong.

I communicate my needs.

I am worthy of love.

I am powerful.

I live in the present.

I see beauty in those I meet.

I accept what I cannot change.

I trust in a Higher Power.

I see love around me.

I give love.

I am love.

I'll fill in my own affirmations here

I am

I am

I am

I am

I am

I am

I

I

I

I

I

I

Congratulations! You have found someone who lights the fire of your desire, a person who makes your eyes twinkle and your voice quiver. Now what?

Try to relax and enjoy every second of this magical relationship, as you savor being in love. Cherish your beloved and allow yourself to be open to the seductive pleasures of *eros*, as the Greeks described the physical attraction between two people. But don't stop there! As you open to love, you will discover the profound and exquisite connection between the spiritual and sexual aspects of love. This is the time to open your heart and soul to another human being, to seek and to be found, to give and to receive love in all its mystery.

Stoke the fires of desire. Allow your partner to know who you really are, as you discover the depths of another soul. As you leave behind the inhibitions that have bound and constricted you in the past, you will feel a sense of power and excitement that will fuel every cell in your body. Your spirit will expand, your heart will grow, and you will feel a connection with those around you. As you give love, so you will receive it. Your glow will inspire others. Waiters will spoil you in restaurants; strangers will smile at you in the street. You will see the world as a happier place and yourself as a kinder, more beautiful person. Love will flow through you and infuse your life with goodness.

Throughout this time, use your journal to go deeply inside and listen to your inner voice. If it's making funny little noises, listen to what it has to say. Ask yourself hard questions. Are you able to be who you are in this new relationship? If not, why not, and what can you do about it? This is a time to be totally honest, for you are laying the foundations for your future relationship with your partner. Try to keep track of your dreams. Often they provide clues as to what the subconscious really feels about a new relationship. Listen to your intuition. If something does not feel right, proceed with caution. If you sense that you are repeating old patterns that you have promised to change, consider this a test of your determination. Finally, if you are convinced that you should be in this relationship, pull out the stops and go for it!

Celebrate by using the creative energy flowing through you. Write poetry. Learn to draw. Buy a set of watercolors. Take up salsa dancing. Wear colors that reflect how you are feeling inside. Create an environment around you that mirrors the way you feel. Be adventurous and go to places you have never been before. In the midst of the whirl, take time to meditate and read books that will inspire and enrich your life.

Above all, be grateful for this opportunity to love and be loved. Use this time to explore the joys of being truly alive—and remember that in love, as in life, the journey is truly the destination!

BUTTERFLIES

I met someone.

Here is how we met

My first impression was

We talked about

I feel

I want to do with you
What spring does
With the cherry trees.
— Pablo Neruda

I just had the most wonderful time.

Here is what happened

I never want to forget

i like kissing this and that of you

— e. e. cummings

DELIRIOUS

I am whirling.

I can't stop thinking about you.

I keep bumping into walls and smiling inappropriately.

I wonder what are you thinking.

I think you are feeling

I am feeling

Lovers don't finally meet anywhere.
They're in each other all along.
— Rumi

I can't sleep. I can't eat. I can't think.

I'm in love!

I always want to remember this feeling.

IN LOVE

When I am in love, I sparkle.

I smile for no apparent reason.

I am generous.

I make other people feel happy just by being around me.

I like myself.

It's funny how other people are attracted to you when you are in love.

Here's how I act when I am in love

I love it when

I wish we could

I want more of

I find it hard to ask for

I need

I would like to try

I want to

I will

BODY & SOUL

I feel like I am merging with you.

Sometimes my feelings are so intense, they scare me.

What is my greatest fear?

How can I deal with it?

I will begin by

if the soul
is to know itself
it must look
into a soul

— George Seferis,
Mythistoreme: Poem IV

It's hard for me to show my feelings.

I learned to bury my feelings when I was

I need to reconnect with my feelings by

I will begin by

Love is not love until love's vulnerable.
— Theodore Roethke, *The Dream*

MIND READER

I can't tell what my partner is thinking.

I am afraid to ask.

What is the worst thing that can happen if I ask?

Last night I dreamed

Here's what I think it means

MORE, PLEASE

Here's what I want from my partner but am afraid to ask for

This is how I feel when I don't get it

Why don't I ask for it?

How could I ask for it?

This is what I will do

Here's what I love about my partner

Here's what I think my partner loves about me

Have we told each other what we feel?

I will begin by

It is one thing to be madly "in love." However, choosing to love is something completely different. Romantic love is based on illusion, while conscious loving is grounded in an "eyes wide open" awareness of your partner as a flesh-and-blood entity, a warped human being shouldering a family history as complex as your own, a real person imbued with hopes and dreams which are as compelling, responding to memories of past relationships that are as confusing.

Committing to love is a monumental undertaking. The mere thought of having to lose independence, being forced to share, giving up personal space, and merging one's life with that of another individual can be so daunting as to make the most brave among us want to run for cover.

Before you flee, though, remember that most of the problems you face can be handled with clear communication. We don't mean the casual language of everyday life, words barely heard against the din of our days, but real listening, hearing, sharing, as we open ourselves to the innermost thoughts of the persons we love. Communication is a two-way street. It's about asking questions and answering them, creating a safe dialogue that respects and empowers two individuals as they journey more and more deeply into the recesses of their hearts, minds, and spirits.

Use the pages in this section to practice being clear and honest about what you feel about your relationship. Identify areas that you think need work and find ways to lovingly express your feelings to your partner. Explore new ways to communicate. Revive the ancient art of writing love letters! In a world of e-mails and hurried phone calls, the sending of an intimate love letter will touch the heart of the recipient infinitely more than even the most well-written e-mail can ever manage.

Above all else, strive to be yourself. In the early phases of a relationship, we can become chameleonlike in our efforts to please our new partners. Once the honeymoon period is over, the shape we have pinched and pulled ourselves to create often sags, and the real us is revealed. That can be a nasty shock for everyone. So, be who you really are and encourage your partner to be true to himself or herself. Be passionate and have fun! This is the time to celebrate your good fortune in knowing and loving each other. Step outside the confines of your daily existence and explore the world around you. Be a bold adventurer, a courageous explorer, and a brave visionary as you create the life of your choice with the person you have chosen to love.

THE PRINCE/PRINCESS FACTOR

I always had an image in my head of my ideal partner.

Now I have someone who doesn't match all the characteristics.

What matters?

○ height

○ looks

○ profession

○ religion

○ the way I feel when we are together

○ sense of humor

○

○

Here is what I think really matters

The heart has its reasons which reason does not know.
— Blaise Pascal

When I am with my partner, do I like who I am?

If not, why not?

Does my partner encourage me to be myself?

Do I become bigger or smaller?

How do I feel inside?

How do I look?

If I am not becoming bigger and truer to myself, there must be something wrong.

I will say what I feel.

Here's how I feel

SEEING THE LIGHT

When someone believes in me and supports my dreams, I feel I can do anything.

Does my partner take time to listen to my dreams?

Am I taking time to listen to my partner's dreams?

Am I supporting my partner's vision?

I will begin by

When people see the worst in me, I give them the worst.

When people see the best in me, I shine.

Today I resolve to see the light in my partner.

I will begin by

SHARING

I am afraid to share this with my partner

Here's why

What's the worst thing that could happen?

What's the best thing that could happen?

Love consists of this, that two solitudes
protect and touch and greet each other
— Rainer Maria Rilke, *Letters to a Young Poet*

Sometimes my partner puts me down and makes me feel small.

I should not have to apologize for being me.

Next time, I will be honest about it when my partner hurts my feelings.

What might I be doing to hurt my partner's feelings?

SPEAKING THE TRUTH

Even if I don't send this letter, I need to get this off my chest.

Dear_____,

Okay, I give up. I can't change what's happening, but I can change how I react to what is happening.

In my relationship, here's what I need to let go of

CHECK LIST

⭕ my partner listens to me

⭕ my partner asks me questions

⭕ I can be completely honest with my partner

⭕ we laugh together

⭕ I can cry

⭕ my partner doesn't judge me harshly

⭕ my partner expresses love freely

⭕ my partner forgives my imperfections

⭕ I am attracted to my partner

⭕ my partner gives good hugs

⭕ my partner encourages me to dream

⭕ my partner respects and encourages my goals

⭕ my partner thinks I am sexy

⭕ I can surrender my inhibition

⭕ my partner is proud of me and tells me so

⭕ I can be who I really am with my partner

⭕

⭕

⭕

⭕

We just don't know how much time we have here. Either of us could be gone tomorrow.

It is so important to tell each other how we feel and never to part in anger.

I must tell you

You still haven't told me

If I died tomorrow, how would you remember me?

If you died tomorrow, how would I remember you?

GIVE & TAKE

The most exciting thing my partner could do for me is

The most exciting thing I could do for my partner is

The sexiest thing my partner could do for me is

The sexiest thing I could do for my partner is

The most loving thing my partner could do for me is

The most loving thing I could do for my partner is

What's stopping me?

I will begin by

In this world of e-mail and instant messaging, we have almost forgotten how to write a love letter.

Today I am going to write you a letter to tell you how I feel.

Dear _____,

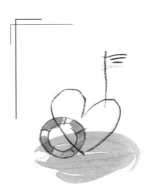

Without love our life is...
a ship without a rudder...
like a body without a soul.
— Sholem Aleichem

HIJACK

We need an adventure

I'm going to hijack my partner and go on a magical mystery tour.

Here is my plan!

We're at the point where we either have to start thinking about a future together or let go.

Here's how I imagine a life with my partner

Here's how I imagine my life without my partner

Which life do I really want?

FREE AT LAST

I never knew how much freedom there could be in commitment.

I always thought I would feel imprisoned in a serious relationship, but because I feel safe,
I feel free—to be me.

Here's how I am reflecting my own true self

Our relationship is working right now.

It seems like one thing flows into another effortlessly.

I want to remember how this feels.

I believe it is happening this way because

When we embark on the journey of conscious loving, we soon realize that the "honeymoon" stage of blind love, while blissful, is only temporary. If we were to remain delirious, with butterflies in our stomachs, we would probably find it difficult to function or hold down jobs. Often, though, when the butterflies have flown, we may not feel ready for the realities and complications of more conscious relationships. In a world of fast foods and quick fixes, we want love to operate just as efficiently. When it doesn't, we are often more inclined to disappear and find someone new than to stick around to sort out the challenges. The problem with leaving is that the cycle begins all over again.

In truth, love is like an endless series of hills and valleys, which—if you think about it—keeps the journey from becoming boring. No matter how long you remain on a particular mountain, there is inevitably a slide down into a new valley, then the long climb up again. That's the way relationships are. "And they lived happily ever after" just doesn't exist in the real world.

When you are in one of the dark valleys, feeling sad, disillusioned, or hurting, it's easy to shrink back and retreat to a quiet place to lick your wounds and cry in peace. That's fine for a while. You need solitude and silence to hear the wisdom of your inner voice to know what to do next.

But then it's time to use your journal to examine what you are feeling. Ask yourself what it is it that is standing in the way of an honest, conscious, open relationship with the person you love. What doesn't feel right? What areas need work? Express yourself on paper and then speak as lovingly as possible to your partner. Evaluate what is lacking in your relationship, then actively seek solutions. Remember, it's a two-way street. Often we are looking for something in others that we really need to find in ourselves.

As you emerge from the delicious honeymoon period, find new ways to express the love you feel for your partner, for a friend, a neighbor, a family member, or a colleague. Remember to express to others the love you wish to receive in your life. Give love, and it will flow back to you. Every valley holds the chance for growth, for learning and new understanding of yourselves and your partner. When it is time to climb out of the valley and trek towards the next mountaintop, you will find you are stronger, wiser, and kinder, and far more able to enjoy the beauty of the view.

POWER SHIFT

There has been a shift in our relationship.

In the beginning it was like this

Now it is like this

We are having trouble finding balance.

I will communicate clearly and lovingly how I feel.

I will say

In the initial stage of our relationship, my partner and I were on our best behavior.

We are slipping!

I don't like the way my partner

My partner doesn't like the way I

Here's what we can work on together

Here's what I can learn to accept about my partner

Here's what I would like my partner to learn to accept about me

RED FLAG

From the very beginning, I knew this was going to be an issue

I was right.

I know I can't expect to change my partner, so can I live with it?

If not, what can I do?

Sometimes I have doubts about my relationship.

Here are some of them:

What can I do to dispel my fears?

I will begin by

CASTLE WALLS

Dear _____ ,

We aren't talking. It is like we are wearing heavy armor, living in cold castles, separated from each other by huge walls and deep moats.

One of us will have to relent and lower a drawbridge.

I'll begin by

I wish you would start by

It's an old trick, but it still works.

Rather than lashing out when my partner makes me mad, I will count to 10 and try to be nice.

Then I will watch what happens to our relationship.

DISTANCE

I'm buried in this relationship.

I need to step back and look at it from all sides.

Here's what I see

Here's what I need to do

Some people try to possess the people they love.

It happened to me when

I felt

If it starts to happen again, I will

Do I smother the person I love?

> You love so much you want to put me in your pocket
> and I shall die there, smothered.
> — D.H. Lawrence, *Sons and Lovers*

MAKES ME CRAZY!

Here are some of my partner's irritating habits

Here are some of mine

Maybe we can make a deal. I'll try to give up my most irritating tendencies, if you will give up yours.

I'll start by

Maybe you could start by

It feels like we talk about this relationship more than we experience it.

Let's try to get through a day just living the relationship lovingly.

Our issues right now are

For God's sake hold your tongue, and let me love.
— John Donne, *The Canonization*

O B S T A C L E S

I know I blame my partner for holding me back.

What is really keeping me from moving forward?

Is it possible that I am the one to blame?

If that's true, then what can I do?

We have gotten into the habit of disagreeing.

I will look at what's happening from my partner's point of view and ask my partner to step into my shoes.

Here's my point of view

Here's my partner's point of view

Maybe if we take the time to understand each other's point of view,
we can be more peaceful with each other.

H I D I N G

Part of me is still holding back. Why?

To feel safe, I need to

My partner needs to

I will begin by

We need to communicate better.

When my partner is honest, here's how I usually react

Instead, I could

When I am honest, my partner usually

It would be better if my partner

Here's what I can do to help us communicate more honestly and clearly

SEEING RED

When I get angry, I

It would be better if I

Next time, I will

When my partner gets angry, my partner

It would be better for us if we

I will find a peaceful time to tell my partner how I feel.

Dear _____ ,

I am sorry.

SOUL FIRE

We need to keep the spark alive.

We need spontaneity in our relationship.

We need romance.

We need excitement,

and giggles,

and lots and lots of love.

To rekindle the fire of our desire I will

I would like you to

Keep me from going to sleep too soon
Or if I go to sleep too soon
Come wake me up.
Come any hour
Of night. Come whistling up the road.
Stomp on the porch. Bang on the door.
Make me get out of bed and come
And let you in and light a light.
Tell me the northern lights are on
And make me look. Or tell me clouds
Are doing something to the moon
They never did before, and show me.
See that I see. Talk to me till
I'm half as wide awake as you
And start to dress wondering why
I ever went to bed at all.
Tell me the walking is superb.
Not only tell me but persuade me.
You know I'm not too hard persuaded.

— Robert Francis, *The Sound I Listened For*

We never think it will to happen to us. When we fall in love, we figure there may be rocky stretches, but we don't plan on the really hard times, when the pain of love gone wrong throws us off balance, threatens our self-esteem, and destroys our peace of mind. As we grapple through the dark tunnel of despair, we often ask ourselves, why, if we once loved each other so deeply, must we hurt each other so much? What can we do to feel better again? How can we find a loving way through the darkness?

There is often truth in the old saying, "Rejection is God's protection," and what we think is a disaster can turn out to be one of life's greatest gifts. It is easy to say that but how do we actually travel through our tortured feelings of anger, betrayal, depression, jealousy, or obsession to find peace and calm? How do we use unimaginable sorrow to strengthen us and focus our energies on a better tomorrow? How can we go through the hard times and remain loving to our partners and ourselves?

This section is devoted to helping you express your deepest, darkest feelings about the person you are meant to love. Putting our angry thoughts into words can be difficult for those of us who habitually deny our true feelings. Often we try to suppress our emotions. We sedate ourselves with antidepressants and gorge ourselves with food, literally swallowing our anger. We drown our sorrows, exercise obsessively, or find escape in drugs, affairs, or just working too hard—anything to numb the pain.

There is a far better way to bring love and peace back into your life. This time, take a moment to retreat to a quiet place. Cry. Rage. Scream. Then write or draw your feelings in your journal, using crayons or magic markers to help you express your hurt or frustration. Don't hold back. This is a safe place to be honest with yourself. As you write, surrender to the wisdom inside you, the limitless, eternal loving energy that is there to help you flow through the heavy emotions.

Breathe, meditate, and find counselors or spiritual mentors to help you on the journey. Cultivate new friends, volunteer, exercise, drink lots of water, and nourish your body, your mind, and your spirit. You will get through this, and one day you will look back and understand what really happened and why, but for now there is no way out but through. Although your partner may be angry, do your best not to retaliate. Either find a way to heal the relationship or leave it. Forgive and move on. No matter what, acknowledge the humanity of the other person and seek the highest, most loving solution for both of you. Throughout this period, always remember "this too shall pass" and strive to look forward to the day that you will emerge from the tunnel, blinking in the light.

H U R T I N G

I feel sore, like an open wound.

Here's what happened

I want to feel better.

Here's what needs to happen

This is what I will do to help myself heal and feel loving again

I am consumed with worrying. I think it's affecting my relationship.

My biggest fears are

Here are the small worries

I will deal with the big fears by

I will handle the small ones by

NEGLECTED

I feel alone.

I hurt inside.

I need to be kind to myself.

I need to reach out and ask for help.

I will begin by

Something is holding me back from my relationship.

It's buried deep inside.

I need help in uncovering it.

I will start by

GREEN-EYED MONSTER

I am possessed by jealousy.

I feel out of control.

I want to

Right now I need to create a safe space around me so I won't do anything stupid.

I won't make snap judgments.

I will stand back from

I will approach this situation from a place of love, not anger.

I will begin by

O! beware, my lord, of jealousy;
It is the green ey'd monster which doth mock
The meat it feeds on.
— William Shakespeare, *Othello*

WIDE OPEN

My heart is broken.

I need to mend it.

I cannot control my partner's behavior, but I can control mine.

I will give love to those around me, knowing that by giving away love, I shall receive it.

It may not be the love I think I need, but it will help me heal.

I will begin by

It is said that hearts are meant to be broken...open.

If that's true, what can I learn from this experience?

I am furious.

I feel like doing something terrible.

I want to

The loving thing to do right now is

I will

There can be no great love without great pain.

— Anonymous

BETRAYAL

I feel betrayed.

It happened like this

I want to

To protect myself I need to

I will

I have a secret.

It's a burden to keep it, but I feel like it may cause more harm if I tell my partner.

I need help.

I will

Oh, what a tangled web we weave
When first we practice to deceive!
— Sir Walter Scott

P A S S I O N   A N D   P A I N

I always wanted passion, but I didn't know about the pain.

Here's what happened

I have to get through this.

I will

⭕ call a friend

⭕ go for a walk

⭕ meditate

⭕ pray

⭕ read an inspirational or spiritual book

⭕ listen to music

⭕ help someone who is in worse shape than I am

I know everyone has a dark side.

When I am in a relationship and the darkness appears in my partner, I feel

To deal with the darkness, I need to

I will begin by

If I feel myself becoming overwhelmed, I will

The soul would have no rainbow if the
eyes had no tears.
— Native American saying

I DON'T LIKE YOU, BUT I LOVE YOU

Today I really don't like you. I can't stop loving you, but I don't like what you are doing.

Here is what is upsetting me

Here is what I would like you to do instead

Here is what I will do

Today I don't like how I feel when I am with you.

This is what you are doing

This is what I would like you to do

This is what I will do

I need to carve out some space, and then we need to do something together which reminds us why we were together in the first place.

SPEAKING THE TRUTH II

Even if I don't send this letter, I need to get this off my chest.

Dear_____ ,

Mahatma Gandhi once said, "If you want to see the brave, look at those who can forgive. If you want to see the heroic, look at those who can love in return for hatred."

Should I be brave?

Should I be heroic?

I NEED HELP

I know there are places I can get help, but I don't like the idea of anyone knowing what's going on.

What's the worst thing that can happen if I seek help?

What's the best thing that can happen?

I will begin by

I know either we must create a loving, caring, nurturing relationship, or we must no longer be together.

Whatever we decide to do, I want the way we do it to reflect the highest, kindest, most loving part of me.

We don't have to continue hurting each other.

We can forgive and love in a different way.

I know I can't control the way my partner will react, but I can control my own behavior.

I will begin by

Nothing is lonelier than being in a relationship with someone when communications have broken down. When we feel deprived of love, we can become small, dark, and joyless. Sometimes we rage against the persons we once loved so deeply or just nag. We can seek love elsewhere or simply retreat in a moody silence, pulling our auras tight round us, like a blanket, and wonder if we can ever love another again.

This section will help you create a joyous renaissance in your relationship by working with love and honesty through issues that divide you towards a future that unites and strengthens you, individually and together. It will show you that it is possible to find peace and joy in what was once a debris-strewn battlefield. With love, you can unite again to create new love in your lives and a new life for your love.

Use this section to outline the old hurts that trigger arguments or launch predictable, useless behavior. Practice the loving words you want to say–and write the words you need to hear from your partner. Spend time remembering what brought you together and what now divides you. Be still and really listen inside. Sometimes we blame others for diverting us from our own true paths. Be honest with yourself. If you feel you should be doing something else, talk it over with your partner and together find a way to follow your heart's desire. Be true to yourself in all that you do and all that you are. Find help through a counselor, therapist, minister, rabbi, or other spiritual counselor who can assist you both in clear, effective, and loving communication.

As you work on your relationship, practice being loveable. Work on your body, your mind, and your spirit. Hard as it may be, try to view your partner as his or her highest self. You know that if you perceive someone as inadequate or weak, chances are that's what you'll get: a pathetic, unappealing person. Try seeing a strong, capable, kind person who's doing the best possible, and watch the difference in how your partner acts and feels about you. Give the love you wish to receive—not only to your partner but also to yourself. Strive to forgive each other: let go and let love heal all that has gone before.

As you open your heart, you will release the source of love that flows everywhere around and through you. Use that powerful love energy to revive and enrich your relationship. Nurture and cherish your partner. Be gentle. Say kind things. Plan a grand adventure or declare a "national holiday" just for the two of you. Resolve to do ten things you have never done before. Plant a tree to symbolize your new commitment to one another. Be outrageous! Stay in bed for a weekend and get all your meals delivered, as you dream huge dreams about your future life together. And then promise that from this day forward, you will love each other as though there may be no tomorrow.

R E B I R T H

Dear_____ ,

I want to rediscover you and remember why we started this journey in the first place.

I want us to make a conscious effort to appreciate each other out loud.

I will begin by

It's gonna be a long drag, but we'll make it
— Janis Joplin (attributed)

Dear_____ ,

We have gone through so much together. There's a lot of hurt and pain. For our relationship to thrive, we can't continue to resent each other. Anger is like trash: if you don't take it out, it festers and rots.

In the past I have been angry about

I know you have been angry about

We need to understand the roots of our problems so we don't keep repeating ourselves. Then we need to let go of our anger and forgive.

WORLDVIEW

We see what we expect to see.

If we are angry and violent, then we see anger and violence in others.

If we are sad, we perceive sadness.

If we are joyous and compassionate, the world around us becomes filled with positive energy.

To create a peaceful relationship, we must be peaceful in ourselves.

How can I create a peaceful, compassionate relationship?

I will begin by

I know of only one duty and that is to love.
— Albert Camus, *The Notebooks*

In the craziness of life, I have forgotten so much.

I want to remember how we used to

I want to tell you

I want you to remember

I want you to tell me

TELL ME YOU LOVE ME

I need to hear loving words

I will say loving words

We need to take time to celebrate the fact we have made it this far!

I know you love it when we

So today let's steal away and get lost together.

Here's what we can do

RETURN

Return often and take me,
beloved sensation, return and take me –
when the memory of the body awakens,
and old desire again runs through the blood;
when the lips and skin remember,
and the hands feel as if they touch again.

Return often and take me at night,
when the lips and the skin remember. . .

— C.P. Cavafy, *The Complete Poems of Cavafy*

If I take the time to think about us, I feel

I don't want

I desire

I regret

I fear

I long for

I hate

I love

I will

CHARTING A COURSE

Now is a good time to remember our dreams and to find ways of enabling each other to achieve them.

I have a dream.

Here's how my partner can help me

My partner has a dream.

Here's how I can help my partner make it happen

We have a dream

We have been through so much together, I think we have forgotten how much we mean to each other.

This year I will

Give all to love
Obey thy heart
Friends, kindred, days,
Estate, good fame
Plans, credit and the muse
Nothing refuse.
— Ralph Waldo Emerson, *Give All to Love*

N A T I O N A L   H O L I D A Y

Today I am declaring a national holiday just for us.

We will celebrate it by

Dear _____ ,

I love you.

I love the way

I love it when you

I love it when we

I love going

I love being

I love hearing

I love seeing

I love feeling

I love touching

I love tasting

I love knowing

I love you.

ONE LIFE BEFORE YOU

Now you will feel no rain
for each of you will be a shelter to the other
Now you will feel no cold
for each of you will be warmth to the other
Now there is no loneliness for you;
now there is no more loneliness.
Now you are two bodies,
but there is only one life before you
Go now to your dwelling place,
to enter into your days together.
And may your days be good
And long on the earth.

— Apache Song

Cohen, Alan, *Happily Even After: Can You Be Friends after Lovers?* Hay House. 1999. Offers parting couples guidance and tools to move from pain and separateness to acceptance and peace of mind.

Gattuso, Joan M., *A Course in Love, Powerful Teachings on Love, Sex and Personal Fulfillment.* San Francisco: HarperSanFrancisco, 1997. Practical, wise lessons on how to sustain a loving partnership with your soul mate.

Gawain, Shakti, *Living in the Light: A Guide to Personal and Planetary Transformation,* 2nd rev. ed. Novato, Calif.: New World Library, 1998. A beginner's guide to spiritual growth which includes helpful exercises and techniques to transform our lives.

Gurian, Michael, *Love's Journey: The Seasons and Stages of Relationships.* Boston: Shambhala, 1995. Identifies the four seasons of a relationship and guides the reader through the challenges partners face on their journey, from the "Season of Enchantment" to the "Season of Nonattachment".

Keen, Sam, *To Love and Be Loved.* New York: Bantam Books, 1997. A combination of moving personal stories and poems which explore the importance of empathy and commitment.

Kraus, Richard L., and Andrea Lissette, *Free Yourself from an Abusive Relationship: A Guide to Taking Back Your Life.* Alameda, Calif.: Hunter House, 1999. A practical seven-step program that restores power and gives hope to those who have suffered from abuse.

Lovric, Michelle, *How to Write Love Letters.* New York: Shooting Star, 1996. A beautifully crafted guide for lovers, that includes historical examples and model letters to inspire you to create the perfect love letter.

Owen, David, *Seven Ages: Poetry for a Lifetime.* Middlesex, United Kingdom: Michael Joseph, 1992. A rich anthology of poetry, combining old favorites with wonderful new finds.

Peck, M. Scott, M.D., *The Love You Deserve: 10 Keys to Perfect Love.* Solana Beach, Calif.: Lifepath Publishing, 1998. An illuminating book which provides practical steps to help you find and keep your soul mate.

————, *The Road Less Traveled: A New Psychology of Love, Traditional Values, and Spiritual Growth.* New York: Simon and Schuster, 1978. The classic book looks at the difference between "in love" and committing to love, and provides a new way of confronting the problems we face in our lives.

Schnarch, David, Ph.D., *Passionate Marriage: Love, Sex and Intimacy in Emotionally Committed Relationships.* New York: W.W. Norton, 1997. A book which helps couples confront and overcome sexual and emotional barriers, enabling them to move into a more loving relationship.

Wilde, Stuart, *Affirmations.* Wichita, Kansas: White Dove International, Inc., 1987. Inspiring affirmations for those who need to build their confidence and take back their power.

Williamson, Marianne, *Enchanted Love: The Mystical Power of Intimate Relationships.* New York: Simon & Schuster, 1999. This thoughtful book explores the idea that the true purpose of romantic love is to connect with the spiritual nature at the essence of all beings.